31 Prayers for the Addict I Love: Volume 2
The King James Version

By Frances D. Roberts

Text copyright © 2018
Frances D. Roberts
All Rights Reserved

Scripture quotations: Authorized King James Version (KJV) Holy Bible, Thomas Nelson, Inc. Copyright © 1977, 1984, 2001.

To the God, family and friends that I love: thank you for loving me so well.

In loving memory of Della Marx, who spent 30 years in a wheelchair because of a drunk driver. She now walks the streets of gold.

DAY 1- STRAIGHT TO THE TOP

Loving an addict hurts. There are few things on earth that can leave us feeling more powerless. It doesn't matter how many times we promise ourselves that we will not be hurt again, there is a particular pain in knowing that one you love will do anything to have the object of their desire. Even if it means injury or death. Even if it ruins their future—or yours. Especially when children pay for it.

How can there be peace and goodness in a household ruled by chaos? What is the answer, or is there one? How could this cherished person become such a disaster? How could a loving God allow such pain? The questions haunt us, as does the guilt because we can do nothing (legal) to stop an addict from the thing that is ruining him or her. So where does one turn when a heart is shredded and the lies pile up like dust? What hope is there for a loved one who is bent on self-destruction?

"For I know the thoughts that I think for you, saith the LORD, thoughts of peace, and not of evil, to give you an expected end." (Jeremiah 29:11)

When the Bible puts LORD in all capital letters, it means that is the name of Almighty God, the God who can do whatever He chooses. Some believe that an addict's free will means that he or she is outside the realm of God's power. If God's blessing is only for those who are seeking God, then why does Paul quote Isaiah in Romans 10:20 saying, **"…I was found of them that sought me not; I was made manifest unto them that asked not after me."** God's strength and forgiveness are available to all in both the Old and New Testament. The Book of John, Chapter 3, verses 16 and 17 says, "For God so loved the world that he gave his only begotten Son, that whosoever believeth in him shall not perish, but have everlasting life. For God sent not his Son into the world to condemn the world; but that the world through him might be saved." The world is not known as a place of love and peace, but God loves it.

Some would argue that God has nothing to do with the addict. He resists the proud (James 4:6), and if there is any creature on earth that is 100% selfish, it is an addict. But those who have "tried everything" are limited by the powers available on earth. So the first prayer goes straight to the top—to the LORD Most High, the All-powerful Creator God, the one who loves us more than we can imagine. If there is one thing that can break the power of even the most entrenched evil, it is the One who broke the power of sin and gave all those who believe abundant life. Read John 3 again, but this time read verses 14 to 17. Jesus was lifted up for us. Almighty God left heaven and came to suffer every indignity we did—without air conditioning, a four-door sedan, or indoor plumbing. He did that for people who were not looking for him or interested in his message. He did that for you, for me, and for the addict(s) we love.

Dear Father in Heaven,
Thank You LORD for showing me what true love is, and for loving me more than I can even imagine. I come before You because I love _____. I know that you love _____ even more than I do, and the things that are breaking my heart break Your heart even more. I believe that nothing can separate us from the love of God, and that You can reach down and heal the one I love. You healed the paralyzed man because his friends had enough faith to break through a roof to get him to You. Lord, I believe. Help my unbelief! Please heal, and restore to us what the locust has eaten. Let _____ acknowledge you as Lord and Savior, and lead him/her in Your ways. Break the chains of addiction. Give _____ life, and abundant life, overflowing with your love. In Jesus' precious name I pray. Amen.

DAY 2 – PRAY EVEN WHEN YOU CAN'T PRAY

Sometimes the pain of loving an addict is so deep that there are no words left to pray. Deceit is as old as the Garden of Eden, and addicts are usually masters at deceiving themselves as well as those who love them. They are also masters at doubling the workload of those who love them—nothing is their responsibility. Of course, it is all about them and what they need. But eventually, the truth comes out. Perhaps you have just been broad sided by the consequences of your loved one's addiction—or even by the knowledge that s/he is an addict. Maybe you have just listened to the last lie in pile of lies that could fill a football stadium, or you dream of crawling inside of his or her brain so you can "fix" the problem. As long as your loved one breathes, there is still hope. Instead of giving up, it is at these times when we must let the Holy Spirit pray for us.

"Likewise, the Spirit also helpeth our infirmities: for we know not what we should pray for as we ought: but the Spirit itself maketh intercession for us with groanings which cannot be uttered. And he that searcheth the hearts knoweth what is in the mind of the Spirit, because he maketh intercession for the saints according to the will of God. And we know that all things work together for good to them that love God, to them who are the called according to his purpose."(Romans 8:26-28)

You may be thinking that you are no saint, and your loved one certainly isn't either. But all those who follow Jesus are saints. God looks at you and sees his Son because you are His. God loves us for the same reason we love our children; they are ours. Love is not conditional. It separates the actions from the person without condoning the wrong. It may feel like our prayers are hitting the ceiling and go no further, but emotions change. God is faithful to listen to our prayers and work all things together for good for those who love Him. When my son was eighteen months old, he started this game in which he'd suddenly throw his head back without warning as he sat on my lap. His head hit me squarely in the mouth drawing blood, and it really hurt. Later that day, he did it again. The pain in my lip was so great that I had to put him down quickly and run to the bathroom before I did something I'd regret. Thankfully, he realized that slamming the back of his head into my lip caused me to put him on the floor instead of my lap, and he stopped doing it. The addict I love, however, was not so concerned with whether or not I held him. Although his idea of love was not selfless, mine must be. As much as I wanted to hate him, I knew that it would not stop the pain in my heart one bit. My ideas of romantic love shattered into a thousand pieces, and I realized that true love was not Cinderella on the dance floor staring wide-eyed at her prince, it was her scrubbing the floor again after the cat made muddy footprints all over it—without pouring her bucket of dirty water over his mean little head.

Whether your reaction to being undone is anger, control, or depression, you must realize that what you hate is the action and that love and revenge cannot exist together. Patience and joy feel impossible when the addict you love is wallowing in foolishness, and it is truly an affliction that keeps on afflicting. Even after years of being clean, an addict can return to the same destructive cycle without warning. It is war, and a war that never ends for them or the people who care about them. Jesus invited those who labor and are heavy burdened to come to Him, he promises to give us rest. Are you so war-weary that you have nothing left? The only answer is prayer--and you don't even have to do it yourself.

Dear Father in Heaven,
I come before you because I love _____. But today it hurts too much to pray. I have no words left inside, only a numbing pain that cuts through me. How long, oh Lord? How many times? Help me to be patient, especially when it hurts. Help me to hate the evil and let my hope for the future bring me joy. Help me to honor the one I love when I want to despise him/her for being so weak AGAIN. Help me to be faithful to pray every time my thoughts turn to this sad situation. Break the chains of addiction. Let _____ feel your love surrounding him/her. In Jesus' precious name I pray. Amen.

DAY 3 - THE LORD'S PRAYER

Matthew 6:9-13 (Jesus said,) "After this manner therefore pray ye: Our Father which art in heaven, Hallowed be thy name, Thy kingdom come, Thy will be done in earth, as it is in heaven. Give us this day our daily bread. And forgive us our debts, as we forgive our debtors. And lead us not into temptation, but deliver us from evil: For thine is the kingdom, and the power, and the glory forever. Amen.'"

I have never wanted to talk to God face to face more than when I realized all the damage the addict I love had wrought in our home, in our finances, and in our relationship. Unfortunately, I have not gotten that one-on-one conversation with the Almighty. From what I've read when Job took a crack at asking God why bad things happen, it didn't go so well for him. God never did answer directly, but He reminded Job of His greatness. Job's story is very frustrating because even though God gave him back twice what he lost afterward, Job still had lost nearly everything he loved. His first set of children never reappeared. God let it happen, and he let it happen to a man who was so righteous that He bragged on Job to Satan.

I know Job's righteousness exceeded mine, and I am not ready to lose my children, so this story shakes me to the core—much like loving an addict shakes me to the core. So if God isn't going to answer me, what is this whole prayer thing about? Jesus answers some of these questions when his disciples asked Him how to pray. Jesus replied with the prayer that is quoted even by people who do not consider themselves devout, who may not know the love and power of God personally. So let's look at each part of this prayer, and see how it helps us when we want answers from God.

*"Our Father in heaven" reminds us that not only is God our loving father, (especially important to those whose earthy father wasn't the greatest or worse) but He is also in a position higher than ours. He reigns in the place of perfect love and peace where every tear will be wiped away. He can see things that we cannot. He has perspective

that we do not have, and He fills the glorious eternity that we look forward to.

* "Hallowed be thy name" says that even God's name is holy and should be honored. Think of those whose names we honor, and the character traits that made them honorable. That is who we are talking to, the honored One who is working all things together for our good.

* "Thy kingdom come" reminds us that this life is not all there is. The sadness and pain we are experiencing is only temporary, and our true kingdom waits for us—our mansion on streets of gold still exists whether we feel rich or not.

* "Thy will be done on earth" seems to clash with the fact that people have free will, and that many use their will for negative purposes. But God can weave even the most frayed threads of broken lives into something beautiful. This is where that maddening patience thing comes in again. God's timing isn't ours. His will wins in the end, but for now we have to accept that God's will is the destination while our journey continues.

*"As it is in heaven" reminds us that there is future with no pain coming. In fact, the glories of heaven are so wonderful that Paul with all his verbosity could not describe it. We have a reason to hope even when things look their bleakest. In the midst of darkest despair, we can know that the glories of heaven wait.

*"Give us this day our daily bread" reminds us that God is our Provider. Maybe the addict you love has left you in such a bad financial position that you don't know where your next meal is coming from. Maybe you have been humiliated by having to accept the charity of a friend or a food pantry. Bankruptcy, bill collectors and bad credit may haunt you, but God knows what you need, and He will provide it today. Ask him for wisdom to find your way out of the situation and listen for an answer. God is still in the miracle business.

*"Forgive us our debts" does not necessarily refer to money. It can also mean those wrongs that we have done. It becomes easy to heap

blame once we have been betrayed and lied to repeatedly. But let's face it: none of us is perfect. We have all wronged somebody at some time. Asking our loving Father for forgiveness reminds us to be humble and to do our best to heal instead of hurt—even when we are frustrated beyond belief and our anger is perfectly understandable by human standards. When we are hurt, we want justice. But when we do wrong, we want mercy. The Lord's Prayer helps us remember the mercy that was and is given to us.

*"As we forgive our debtors" is one of the hardest things we are asked to do. How can we forgive *again* when the lies pile up like leaves in the fall? God forgives us when we ask, but He does not condone the wrong. Sin has consequences, and we must not fall into the trap of minimizing them when our loved one falls. Forgiveness does not say that wrong is okay or help to promote wrong. Forgiveness simply says, "Debt cancelled. You owe me nothing. No payment required." Bitterness will eat an unforgiving person alive, and there are enough battles to fight in this life without adding to them. Even if the addict you love doesn't ask, forgive him or her as God forgives you.

*"Deliver us from evil." The devil roams about like a roaring lion looking for one to devour. He knows just how to make poison look enticing. Pray that this lion won't devour you or yours, and will stop feasting on the addict you love. It can be so hard to have faith when loss and heartbreak surround us, but we must believe that our loving Father has a plan for each life, and that He will hear the prayers for those who we love.

Dear Father in heaven, Hallowed be thy name. Thy kingdom come, may your will be done on earth as it is in heaven. Give us this day our daily bread. Forgive us our debts, as we have forgiven our debtors. And lead us not into temptation, but deliver us from the evil one. Please break the chains of addiction, and heal _____.
Amen.

DAY 4- THE REAL ENEMY

Addiction can make the sweetest person do heartless things. We know that even when they break our heart and make our lives difficult, our enemy is not the one we love.

"For we wrestle not against flesh and blood, but against principalities, against powers, against the rulers of the darkness of this world, against spiritual wickedness in high places."(Ephesians 6:12)

There are several enemies mentioned here, and none of them exist in the physical realm. So how do we fight the untouchable? We need more than good intentions; we need armor. Ephesians 6:13-18 gives us the armor we need, and not only us, but the ones we love also.

"Wherefore take unto you the whole armour of God, that ye may be able to withstand in the evil day, and having done all, to stand. Stand therefore, having your loins girt about with truth, having on the breastplate of righteousness; and your feet shod with the preparation of the gospel of peace; above all, taking the shield of faith, wherewith ye shall be able to quench all the fiery darts of the wicked. And take the helmet of salvation, and the sword of the Spirit, which is the word of God: praying always with all prayer and supplication in the Spirit, and watching thereunto with all perseverance and supplication for all saints..."

These verses teach several lessons. It takes the strength of God to stand when most people would flee. Usually when there is a reference to girding oneself, a person is either getting ready to fight or perform an important task. As somebody who loves an addict, the language of the liar is like a slap in the face. It hurts. So if the truth is how we prepare ourselves, it must be important. Are you lying to yourself about something? Is there a way you can tell the truth and still protect yourself? Righteousness is your refuge. It is so easy to lash out when angry or afraid. Sometimes the easy way can actually hurt the one you are trying to protect. Getting used to speaking the truth in love and doing what is right isn't weakness; it is what preserves you. It is the easiest thing in the world to cut somebody to ribbons when they've let you down. Get to know God's word; you can't march very far when your feet are all torn up. The word of God also is your sword, a two edged sword that cuts both ways. That's a powerful weapon when you're fighting for your life. Your faith and your salvation will protect your head and your body, and everything else will be covered through prayer. Get close to Almighty God. He is your protector and deliverer. He will fight for you if you let Him. Ask Him when you need to fight and when you need to flee. He will show you how to use your weapons when you need them if you only ask. And just maybe by watching you use your Spiritual repertoire, the addict you love will learn to fight from a position of strength too.

Dear Father in Heaven,
Thank You for showing me how to stand in the face of overwhelming attacks, even when I feel completely beaten down. Help _____ to stand as well. Break the chains of addiction. Help us not to become battle weary. Help the past not to stop me or _____ from doing what is right. Take old hurts away, so we can fight each battle one day at a time. Protect us from the enemy, Lord. Give _____ the truth and righteousness that come from being filled with the Holy Spirit. Help us to learn your word, so the good news (gospel) will fill us with truth and hope. Give us the faith to quench anything thrown our way. Cover us with your salvation and fight this battle against powers that we cannot defeat on our own. Help us to watch, to persevere, and to pray. Give us hope, even when the battle looks lost, and break the chains of addiction. Thank You for life, an abundant life, overflowing with your love. In Jesus' precious name I pray. Amen.

DAY 5- LOVE IS NOT A FEELING

Romans 13:8 Owe no man any thing, but to love one another: for he that loveth another hath fulfilled the law.

You may have laughed out loud when you saw the part about owing no debt. Loving an addict can be the most expensive venture that you have ever undertaken. Worse, you may not have discovered how expensive until it was too late to fix it. But anger and hatred won't fix it either. The purpose of the law is to teach us right from wrong. If love fulfills the law, it must be the greatest thing; Jesus even said that it was. Sometimes the way we see love portrayed in popular culture blinds us to what love really is. Love, Paul says, is patient first. Then love is kind. It takes an almost superhuman patience to love an addict. Watching them destroy their own life (and usually more than just their own life) is painful enough, but then they have the gall to ask you for money to get more poison. Some don't even ask; they just take. For some, that is just the first step in a whole pile of hurtful circumstances that grow incrementally with each encounter, drink, pill or puff. These actions do not lend themselves to kindness. Disappointment, fear and anger may fill your life daily. So how do we separate the evil actions from the person we love? How do we keep from enabling them to hurt others and destroy themselves yet quench the resentment that comes from having to be on guard 24-7-365 with no break in sight? The holidays are often the worst, and the only thing we can be sure of is: we will never be sure.

Romans 12:9-12 Let love be without dissimulation. Abhor that which is evil; cleave to that which is good. Be kindly affectioned one to another with brotherly love; in honour preferring one another; not slothful in business; fervent in spirit; serving the Lord. Rejoicing in hope; patient in tribulation; continuing constant in prayer.

Hating what is evil is not hard to do, but honoring an addict is extremely difficult. How can I respect a self-destructive person? It is hard to be zealous when I am worn out. It is almost impossible to pray with fervor when I'm hearing the same sad song over and over.

I don't feel like I'm serving the Lord, I feel like a mouse on a spinning wheel with no way off of it, and that is not even the hardest part! Why bother working hard when the money will most likely be wasted?

How can I be joyful in hope, when my hopes and dreams have been smashed to powder? There is nothing more maddening than trying to be patient in affliction. Affliction hurts! I don't want to wait any more, and I feel like my prayers are just aimlessly zipping through the universe, unheard and unanswered. Don't let my feelings take me away from Your truth. Help me to keep fighting the good fight.

Dear God Almighty,
I come before you because I sincerely love _____.
Help me to be faithful to pray every time my thoughts turn to this situation, especially when I feel exhausted or furious. Teach me to honor others without prejudice and help us not to lose hope. Help me to be patient especially when it hurts. When I wish I didn't care, help me to care more. When we feel like we have no strength to go on, fill us with Your strength. Don't let us dwell on the past, but to cling to what is good. Let _____ feel your love surrounding him/her and break the chains of addiction. In Jesus' precious name I pray. Amen.

DAY 6- PRAISE DURING THE TEMPEST

Psalm 29:10-11 The LORD sitteth upon the flood; yea, the LORD sitteth King forever. The LORD will give strength unto His people; the LORD will bless His people with peace.

Sometimes loving an addict feels like asking for a hurricane. The winds howl, the rains beat on the roof and it seems like you will never know peace and quiet again. Sometimes the damage is extensive. Other times there are just a few limbs left in the yard. Each time there is the question hanging in the air: how much damage will there be this time, and when is the next storm coming?

God is Lord of the storm, even when it feels like He's sleeping in the boat—or even worse, is not there at all.

Psalm 77:16-19 The waters saw thee, O God, the waters saw thee; they were afraid: the depths also were troubled. The clouds poured out water: the skies sent out a sound: thine arrows also went abroad. The voice of thy thunder was in the heaven: the lightnings lightened the world: the earth trembled and shook. Thy way is in the sea, and thy path in the great waters, and thy footsteps are not known.

It is hard to see how God is working when everything is crashing down around us, but we can be comforted that the One who calmed the storm and raised the dead holds us and our loved ones in His hands.

1 Thess. 5:18 In every thing give thanks: for this is the will of God in Christ Jesus concerning you.

It seems like a ridiculous answer when your heart is breaking, but it works. Read through the Psalms. Often the psalmist begins by pouring out his broken heart to the Lord and ends with praise. Get in the habit of counting your blessings and trusting God. As you praise God, feel the tension leaving your body and praise Him some more. What do you have to lose?

Dear God Almighty,
This storm has me quaking in my boots. The boat is rocking and the water is rising. I'm sinking, Lord, and I don't know if I can make it to shore. I feel so alone, and it seems like this tempest will never end. I can't see any way out, Lord. I am exhausted and discouraged. I have tried everything I can imagine, but there seems to be no hope. But I know that You are with me and the addict I love. I know that we are precious in Your sight, and I will praise You even though things seem hopeless. Break the chains of addiction and heal _____. Heal my heart, and give me strength to follow this course for as long as You would have me follow it. In Jesus' precious name I pray. Amen.

DAY 7 - PRAYER FOR THE CHILDREN

Mark 10:13-14 And they brought young children to him, that he should touch them: and his disciples rebuked those that brought them. But when Jesus saw it, he was much displeased, and said unto them, "Suffer the little children to come to me, and forbid them not: for of such is the kingdom of God."

It is easy for some people to brush children aside, or to tell themselves that they will get over it or that they won't remember. But children are incredibly perceptive, and they know when they are not safe. They can spot a fake faster than many adults, and so they often suffer the rage of the manipulator. I will never forget the first moment that I looked at the tiny face of each of my children. Such love raced through my body that I felt supercharged. I knew that there was nothing in this world that would keep me from protecting them. But there are times when I am impatient or too hard on them. There are times when I fail to give them my best, and I have all my faculties in place. How hard it must be for an addict to put their child's welfare first!

Matt. 18:6 (Jesus said,) "But whoso shall offend one of these little ones which believe in me, it were better for him that a millstone were hanged about his neck, and that he were drowned in the depth of the sea."

God obviously has a great love for children. Unfortunately, human history has shown that often people do not. Children have been killed throughout our history because they were imperfect or inconvenient, because the parents couldn't afford them or because they were at the wrong place at the wrong time. Sometimes they were sacrificed to gods in exchange for prosperity. Death is not the only abuse that children suffer. It is a shame and a tragedy how children are abused and neglected by some people. Even in the best families, children suffer for the sins of their parents. A spoiled child can grow up to be as much of a nightmare as an abused child. It is a hard thing to raise a child properly, to train him up in the way that he should go, without being too lenient or too strict. But even the most loving and conscientious parent cannot touch the depths of love that God has for their child. We have a loving father that we can turn to when we need Him.

Dear Heavenly Father,
Thank You for the gift of my children. Help me to be a blessing in their lives in every way. Bless their future, Lord. Bring people into their lives that love and serve You. Help them to know You as Lord and Savior. Protect the children I love from the dangers in our world. Even when the grow up to do wrong, even when they run the other direction, Lord, I know that You are waiting for them to turn to You and be saved. Father, I think of the children who are hurting because of the addict I love. Wrap Your arms around them and protect them. Provide a way for them to be safe and well cared for. Help me to unselfishly think of them even when I am tired or beaten down. Help me to make wise choices in everything that has to do with them. Break the chains of addiction and heal the addict I love. Heal the children involved in this situation, and let them have peace and comfort. Please don't let the children reap what the parents have sown. Have mercy on us, Lord. Bless us and make Your face shine upon us. Grant us peace. In Jesus' name I pray. Amen.

DAY 8- WHY US, LORD?

Ps. 23:1- The LORD is my shepherd; I shall not want.

But, of course, we want plenty of things. We want peace. We want certainty. We want the addict we love to be healed and stop lying and destroying. We want the shame to go away, especially if we are still hiding the addiction from others. Shining the light on the dark places will not hurt; it will help. Many hands make light work in more things than housework. When we share our burdens with those we love—especially with a trusted prayer partner—we gain an extra set of eyes and praying hands. We need to separate ourselves from the situation and pray and talk with somebody who is not affected by it. It will give us another perspective and much needed down time. Let your prayer partner know that you're not looking for a fixer, just a sympathetic ear who will hear your concerns and pray for them.

One addict I know always had money to buy cigarettes and beer, but he never would get his wife a birthday present or Christmas present. That hurt her more than words can express, and many of her friends encouraged her to move on. But even when the Bible does allow for divorce (for adultery) Jesus says that God allowed it only because of the hardness of our hearts. The Bible says that the Lord hates divorce. So telling the unappreciated wife how quickly she should "dump the loser" isn't going to help her. It may only add to her pain because she may already want to run screaming in the opposite direction. As the child of divorced parents I know how divorce shakes a child's world—and I was grown when my parents divorced. Some things just can't be fixed easily. Sometimes we have to wait on the Lord, and his timing is incredibly slow to our way of thinking—especially when it hurts.

I know a woman who prayed for her alcoholic husband for fifteen years until he bent his knee and decided to let God run things. Two years later, she said that all the waiting was worth it because he had become such a wonderful father and husband. If she had given up on him after fourteen years and eleven months of praying, she and her family would have missed out on so much. Don't quit; God never quit on us.

Proverbs 3:3 Let not mercy and truth forsake thee: bind them about thy neck; write them upon the tablet of thine heart.

Sometimes we take pride in being the victim. As if having the wounds aren't enough, we take them out and examine them, like peeling off a scab or sticking our tongue in the place where a tooth used to be. We want our pound of flesh or just to know that somebody cares that we are hurting.

Dear Father in Heaven,
Sometimes I do want to run screaming in the opposite direction. I am tired of being tired. I am tired of never knowing what awful surprise is waiting around the corner. I am tired of being afraid of coming home to find that the addict I love has disappeared again, or has lost the job again, or of getting that phone call that s/he's been arrested, or the kids have been taken away, or worst of all, that s/he's dead. I don't deserve this. I know that I am blessed with many things, but I don't understand why You think I am strong enough to take this, Lord. I am beaten down and worn out. I have faith that you want what is best for me and for my loved ones, but how long will this go on? How many disappointments? How many broken promises? Deliver me from the pride of life and from being disgusted when the addict I love is weak. Give him/her the strength to turn from the things that are ruining his/her life. I love _____ and I know that You do too. I know You will provide a way out so _____ will not continue to fall into the same old patterns of failure. Give _____ wisdom and break the chains of addiction. In Jesus' name I pray.

DAY 9- LOOKING FOR RIGHTEOUSNESS

Matthew 5:6- *Blessed are they which do hunger and thirst after righteousness: for they shall be filled.*

   If you are only worried about the addict that you love staying straight on his or her own while you walk the fine line between God's will and the world, you probably have a problem. You cannot play with fire and not get burned. Even if you get away with it a dozen times, there is going to be a payday.

Ephesians 5:18- *And be not drunk with wine, wherein is excess; but be filled with the Spirit.*

The wife of an alcoholic husband sat at a dinner party drinking wine with their host, then lit into him as soon as they got home because his shirt smelled like alcohol. Did she think that he wouldn't smell it on her breath? That he wouldn't taste the alcohol when he kissed her? I hope I am never so foolish as to tempt the addict I love with something that will bring him down. Although we cannot "fix" them, there are things that we can do to help them walk away when they are tempted. There are people who we know are toxic to the addict we love. It is especially hard when the toxic people are family, but this is war! And it is war every single day. There are situations that addicts don't need to be placed in. Do you want to be popular or do you want to have the addict you love in one piece? You all ready know that there is no "off" switch once they start. So take precautions to help keep them straight. The addict I love does not have a problem with alcohol, but once he has a few drinks he is weak and ready for anything. So I don't serve him alcohol. There are barriers that you can erect which will help the addict you love stay in the right places. Certainly, s/he must agree. So make a plan together avoid triggers and toxic people. One glass of wine can lead to a whole world of trouble.

   Who hath woe? Who hath sorrow? Who hath contentions? Who hath babbling? Who hath wounds without cause? Who hath redness of eyes? They that tarry long at the wine; they that

go to seek mixed wine. Look not thou upon the wine when it is red, when it giveth his color in the cup, when it moveth itself aright. At the last it biteth like a serpent, and stingeth like an adder. Thine eyes shall behold strange women, and thine heart shall utter perverse things... Proverbs 23:29-33

Dear God Almighty,
Sometimes it makes me so upset because I shouldn't have to be so careful about everything, but loving an addict means that I do. Give me wisdom to do things that will build him/her up instead of tearing down defenses. Please protect us from bad choices. Help us not to take things lightly or let our guard down when we know that _____does not have an "off" button. Help us to hunger and thirst for righteousness. Fill us with your goodness, mercy and self-control. I know that _____ may not be able to go the rest of his or her life without falling prey to addiction, but let _____ do it right today. Let us rejoice in each victory. Let me be a blessing in his/her life and not a hindrance. If I have to give up something that I like to save somebody that I love, let me do it with a happy heart. Thank You for blessing me with _____, whom I love so much. In Jesus' precious name I pray.

DAY 10- WHEN DOES THE HEALING BEGIN?

Jer. 33:3- *Call unto me, and I will answer thee, and show thee great and mighty things, which thou knowest not.*

If people could see the figurative knives from all the times that the addict I love has stabbed me in the back, I would look like a porcupine. The worst thing is, he thinks that the words 'I'm sorry' have magical healing powers and can take away the effects of all his bad choices. Sometimes it seems like the more good things I do for that man the more I am rewarded with heartlessness—no good deed goes unpunished. I wish I could turn into the TV, so he would pay a little attention to me. When I cry out to God I know that He hears me, but it is a rare day that an answer appears. I feel like such a fool sometimes. Other times, when I'm protecting the addict I love from temptation (like not buying items that can be modified into drug paraphernalia) I look like I am the guilty one. One of my brothers told me that I "knew too much". How can I fight something when I'm in the dark? Knowledge is power. Each time he falls, I learn a little more about how he operates, but it is a tedious process. For every addict I know that has overcome an addiction, there is another who is trapped in its vicious cycle.

Phil. 1:6- *Being confident of this very thing, that he which hath begun a good work in you will perform it until the day of Jesus Christ:*

Even though I don't understand God's purpose in all of this, I know that He has a perfect plan. I fear that part of it is trying to teach me patience, and I really don't want to learn. I'd rather be impatient and content. But I believe that all things work together for good for those who love the Lord, and I do love Him.

Phil. 4:13 *I can do all things through Christ which strengtheneth me.*

Dear Father in Heaven,
I am so glad that You care about my problems, and that You have promised to strengthen me when I am weak.

When I don't understand, please wrap Your arms around me and help me to walk worthy of Your name. Even when I'm disgusted and fed up give me the wisdom to do what is right. Let me run after righteousness and away from bitterness. Lord, I know that the addict I love needs to walk with You every day, too. Help him/her to tap into Your strength. Heal _____ and break the chains of addiction. There is enough sorrow in this world, Lord. Help us to be part of the solution, not the problem. Give us wisdom, strength and a sound mind. Give us gentleness, faithfulness and self-control. Nothing is impossible for You, and I am asking you to work a mighty miracle in this situation. Please, Lord, heal us. In Jesus' name I pray. Amen.

DAY 11 - WHO WINS?

John 16:33 (Jesus said,) "These things I have spoken unto you, that in me ye might have peace. In the world ye shall have tribulation: but be of good cheer; I have overcome the world."

Even though I know that God's people win in the end, my heart is beyond broken when it comes to loving an addict. If I counted up all the lies and tried to pay back all the hurt, anger, and broken promises, I could not be successful. Worse, sometimes the addict I love has the guts to insinuate that it is my fault when he chooses to harm himself and put our family at the brink of financial ruin. I just want to scream, "Why don't you grow up? Stop looking for the eternal high, and act like an adult. What is so wrong with reality?" Sometimes I do ask when he will grow up, be a man, stop running away from problems. It never helps. He doesn't see how his choices hurt the people who love him most because many of the people he loves most/works with are also addicts. They condone the behavior and encourage the addict I love to embrace the addiction regardless of its effects on the family. He promised to love, honor and cherish me until death do us part. His children need him to be an example of the Father's love. But there is not a promise that hasn't been broken, and the way he looks me in the eye and lies without blinking makes my heart ache. It's maddening sometimes. Many days it feels like he loves everything more than his family. It feels like the sorrow will crush my joy, and if I let it, it will.

Ps. 34:18 The LORD is nigh unto them that are of a broken heart; and saveth such as be of a contrite spirit.

Dear Father in Heaven,
Heal my crushed spirit and broken heart. Heal all of those who are hurt by this situation, especially _____. Knowing that we will win in the end does not help now when I am surrounded by disappointment, when it feels like my heart has been pounded into dust. It feels like my dreams have been pulverized too. It feels

like the sorrow has overtaken me. Lord, help _____ deal with his/her sorrow, disappointment and pain also. Heal us, Lord. Restore what has been taken from us. Restore our peace, our hope, and our joy. I know that You have a plan, and that there is a reason that we are walking through this. Give us patience and self-control. Break the chains of addiction and heal _____. I know that you love us more than we can imagine. Wrap your arms around us and comfort us. Help us to celebrate each victory and attack each defeat with prayer. Lord, I know this is not a sprint; it's a marathon. Give us the endurance to run the whole race. Don't let us quit, but let us have the victory. When we tire, strengthen us. In Jesus' name I pray. Amen.

DAY 12- TIME OF REFRESHMENT

Luke 5:16 And he (Jesus) withdrew himself into the wilderness, and prayed.

Why would the Son of God need to separate himself from the crowd and pray? What is the purpose of this when Jesus admitted that God always heard and answered him? Could it be that this is an example of how important it is for us to stop being busy and be alone with God? It is a stressful thing to love somebody who is bent on self-destruction. It makes our already busy lives more difficult. Despite our best efforts and intentions, we get worn down from repeatedly experiencing one disappointment after another or from wondering when the next manmade disaster will happen.

Psalms 40:1-3 I waited patiently for the LORD; and He inclined unto me, and heard my cry. He brought me up also out of an horrible pit, out of the miry clay, and set my feet upon a rock, and established my goings. And he hath put a new song in my mouth. Even praise to our God: many shall see it, and fear, and shall trust in the LORD.

Wouldn't it be wonderful if the addict you love could pray that victory prayer today? How nice for him or her to be walking on solid rock with a song of praise on his or her lips! It would refresh everyone who has come into contact with the situation and be an incredibly powerful testimony of God's love. It is true that one day our loved ones will all be healed—on this side of the grave or the other. However, that is not much comfort when we are in the middle of a huge mess created by an addiction or when we can only stand on the sidelines and watch people we love fall apart. We must be faithful to take time away from all the stress and busyness of our day to spend time alone with our loving Father.

Think about the people that you love, and how empty your life would be without their company or comfort. The Lord loves you infinitely more than you can imagine. Spend time in His company. Talk to Him and pour out your heart to the King of Kings. Make time to do it. You will not be sorry. Don't just do it for the addict you love; do it for yourself.

Dear Father in Heaven,
I know that you love me more than my mind can comprehend. I know that you love me simply because I am Yours, and that there is nothing I have to do to earn Your love. I know that you love _____ more than any mind can comprehend. I know that you love him/her simply because s/he is Yours, and that there is nothing s/he has to do to earn Your love. Help us to rest in that knowledge, Lord. Help us to turn to You each day with our hopes, fears, and praise. Thank You for letting us find strength and refreshment in Your presence, especially when things are toughest. Let us remember that You are more than my best friend, You are the God of all creation and there is nothing that is impossible for You. Give us peace, Lord. Give us rest from the troubles that plague us. Heal the addict I love and restore the years that the locust has eaten. Break the chains of addiction, Lord, and comfort all of us who are hurting. Help the addict I love to learn to lean on You when life hurts, and help me to be the example of this to him/her. In Jesus' name. Amen.

DAY 13- WHEN DEATH SEEMS LIKE A WELCOME BREAK (1 KINGS 17)

Elijah was fed by ravens and lived with a widow during a terrible drought. He raised her son from the dead. God miraculously fed the three of them from a jar that would not run out of flour or oil until the rains came. Though Elijah was a hunted man, he had the guts to stand up to one of the wicked king and queen combinations of all time, and defeated the 450 false prophets of Baal. He saw a water-soaked sacrifice consumed by heaven's fire. Then he ran for his life. He went from the highest high to the lowest low. He prayed that he would die, thinking that he was utterly alone. Sound familiar? Everything is going great, and then Bam! Chaos reigns. You finally believe that life is going to be smooth sailing for a change and your sails fall flat and the sharks are circling.

But God fed Elijah and gave him rest. He reminded Elijah that he was not alone, but there were 7,000 men who had not bowed their knee to Baal. (This is recorded in 1 Kings chapters 17-19.) God loved and cared for His prophet Elijah. There was another prophet who prayed for death, but this time it was in the throes of a temper tantrum. Jonah was furious that God had spared Nineveh instead of destroying them for their wickedness. He did not recognize God's mercy when a large plant shaded him as he sat in the blazing sun, waiting to see the destruction of thousands of people. Jonah did not die, and God reminded him that people, even evil people, are still precious to Him. God loves His enemies in many ways throughout Scripture, which sets Him apart from any god this world can concoct.

    I wonder how many times I think I'm being Elijah (just plain exhausted) when I'm really being Jonah (furious that God doesn't punish the wicked in my time, my way). I wonder if the addict I love realizes what mercy has been poured out for him, though he drags God's name through the mud every time he runs to his first love. I hate to think of how often I am beaten down and my actions don't show the love of God, but the temper tantrum of Jonah the cowardly prophet.

Dear Father in Heaven,
I am really, really exhausted. I would like to sleep forever sometimes. Please give me comfort and rest. Feed me with your word, and give me what I need. I don't know how You can watch all the evil You see and still love us. I honestly don't. I love my children dearly, but when one of them hurts another it really raises my ire. I know that You are angry with the wicked every day, but I also know that Your mercy is unparalleled; You give us more time than we deserve to turn back to You. Help the addict I love to run from evil, to forgive the past hurts, to live his or her life in the joy of the Lord. For those who were introduced to their addiction in the womb, please heal them from the sins of their mothers and fathers. Heal my children from the penalty my sins put on their lives as well. Don't let me ever fall into despair or self-righteousness, but break the chains of addiction holding the addict I love. Help those I love to never bow their knee to false idols. Help us to live in the light, in Your truth. In Jesus' name I pray. Amen.

DAY 14- WHAT CAN JOB'S SUFFERING TEACH US?

Job 1:7-8 And the LORD said unto Satan, Whence comest thou? Then Satan answered the LORD and said, From going to and fro in the earth, and from walking up and down in it. And the LORD said unto Satan, Hast thou considered my servant Job, that there is none like him in the earth, a perfect and an upright man, one that feareth God, and escheweth evil?"

Obviously, God knew exactly where Satan had been, but the information recorded in these verses tells us several things. Satan cannot exist in more than one place. He had to walk from place to place; he is not omnipresent like God. He is limited. Also, we see that God asks Satan to consider Job. Why? Satan is cast out of heaven and doomed. What would be the purpose of him considering a righteous man, since Satan cannot be saved? God knew that Satan would try to show that Job only served God because he had been greatly blessed, but God used Satan's challenge to show us that sometimes a terrible tragedy has no earthly explanation.

At times we are tested in spite of being faithful. We know that Job ended up with double blessings from God after his time of testing was over, but that seems small comfort after losing ten beloved children, thousands of cattle, his health, and his home. What was God thinking?

Job's first answer to all of this tragedy is astounding. He says, "Naked came I out of my mother's womb, and naked shall I return thither: the LORD gave, and the LORD hath taken away; blessed be the name of the LORD." He blessed God after losing almost everyone he loved, and God further let Satan attack him? It actually got worse for Job after he made that incredible statement of faith. If Satan can viciously attack a righteous man like Job, what hope is there for regular people or especially for the addicts we love? Instead of helping him, even Job's friends accused him. Everything seemed to be against Job, and then when he cries out to God he gets no answers to his questions. Instead, he is humbled.

Did you ever consider that it is pride that has to have answers for everything? We always feel like we have to do something, to somehow "fix" the addict we love. But in our hearts we know that there is nothing we can do to fix the situation. The addict we love must want to quit. There is only One who can change a heart. We have to learn to trust God. So does the addict we love. The enemy we are fighting is not all-powerful or omnipresent, but the God we serve is.

***Dear LORD Almighty,**
We know that You have the power to do anything, but that Your ways are higher than our ways. Show us the lessons You are trying to teach. Help us to rely on Your strength, especially when things make no sense. Give us the faith of Job, the wisdom of Solomon and the heart to seek your will. This life is only temporary, Lord. Help me to remember that this suffering is only for a short time, and that You have a purpose for it. Heal the addict I love, and break the chains of addiction. I don't understand, but I trust You. I hate the pain, but I trust You. Every day I want to trust You more. Heal _____ and show him/her your power and love. In Jesus' precious name I pray. Amen.*

DAY 15- I'M TOO ANGRY TO PRAY FOR THE ADDICT I LOVE

Most people can't picture Jesus destroying the tables of the money changers in the temple. He had no patience with those who drove people away from God. I am so angry that I could braid a whip and throw over some tables myself. Help me to use this anger to do Your will. Maybe it won't be today or even tomorrow, but help me to do it Your way, even when I don't want to. Lord, let this nightmare be over soon!

Ephesians 4:26 *Be ye angry, and sin not: let not the sun go down upon your wrath:*

Dear Father in Heaven,
I am angry, disgusted and sick of it! I am sick of the heartache, the lies, and the children who are suffering—all of it. Solomon said that if you grind a fool with a mortar and pestle, still the foolishness will not leave him. So what is the use of trying anymore? I am sick and tired of being in the dark, of being taken for granted, of being the responsible one. I am sick of never knowing when the next shoe will fall. I hate that we don't matter. I am so angry that I could spit nails, and without Your help, I probably could do something that will land me in jail. It is all so unfair, Father. It has gone on for too long. You are Almighty—all mighty. You can do anything. You said if we ask, believing, we shall receive. I'm tired of asking. I'm tired of

loving somebody so willing to run toward destruction, so selfish, so thoughtless. I am furious, and the sun just better stand still in the sky if it can't go down while I'm angry. Lord, I cannot pray for _____ today. Please have your Spirit do it for me. I am glad that You forgive freely, but You are God. I am just a person, and I have had enough. I am done for today, and I am going to sleep. Please let me have a time of peace and rest. Please give _____ what s/he needs today. Heal this situation and my broken heart. Heal our family. Break the chains of addiction and do a mighty miracle for the addict I love. In Jesus' name I pray. Amen.

DAY 16- DEATH IS DEFEATED?

A good man died, and as I heard all the people talk during his memorial service about what a great effect he'd had on their lives, I grieved for the addict I love. This man was a volunteer with Celebrate Recovery, and I knew that addiction had touched his life in some way. But the man was as selfless as any I had known. He had gotten so much joy out of serving others, and helped so many at the same time. The addict I love is not interested in serving. His children will likely have to work very hard to come up with some good memories. His co-workers will say he was a nice enough guy and got the job done, but not much else. Not many can say that they served with him in church or that he told them about the power of God. The television that he spent so many hours watching will be silent. The people he ran to when he had money in his pocket wouldn't grace the doors of any church much less reach out to others in faith. What a waste that he buried his talent in the ground when he could have done so much good. God has given us all unique gifts, but one gift he makes available to all—eternal life with Him. Because of this we should never be puffed up with pride, and because of this there is always hope for the addict I love.

Ezekiel 18:32 For I have no pleasure in the death of him that dieth, saith the Lord GOD: wherefore turn yourselves and live ye.

Death is not only defeated, but also death is only the end of our life on this earth. There is a heaven waiting for us that is so glorious that Paul with all his words could not describe it. But there is also a payday for some who go their own way. Actions have consequences. Ananias and Sapphira told one lie and they died immediately, while some people mock God for decades and seem to live prosperous lives. It just doesn't seem fair.

When you love an addict, the specter of death may often rear its ugly head. It is scary and stressful to know that you love somebody who is playing Russian Roulette with his or her life. God has given us free will, but it is clear that He would rather that we live and walk with Him.

Dear LORD Almighty,

We know that death was defeated when Jesus rose again, but there is a very real possibility that death may be coming early to the addict I love. Only You can rescue _____ from bad choices. A body can take only so much abuse, and the kind of people surrounding _____ are not healthy. I know that there is sin leading to death, but I also know that you are a God of mercy, who desires that none should perish. Help _____ to make choices that will allow him/her to live a full life, and to be here for those who love him/her. Help the children and all the innocents connected to this situation to find peace and rest securely in Your love. Help me not to enable the addict I love to wallow in the addiction in any way. Please heal the addict I love, and break the chains of addiction. Heal _____ and snatch him/her from the arms of death. Show him/her your power and love in a mighty way. In Jesus' precious name I pray. Amen.

DAY 17- I'M TIRED OF BEING STRONG

***Blessed is that man that maketh the LORD his trust, and respecteth not the proud, nor such as turn aside to lies.
Psalm 40:4***

It is the hardest thing in the world to show respect to an addict. We know that person is a slave to his or her addiction in every way. We know that the addict(s) we love will do almost anything to get the thing that they desire most. When the consequences come, s/he will lie about it without blinking.

I often wonder what went on in Jesus' mind when he was being repeatedly snubbed by the church leaders of his day. He rarely corrected them or told them what he thought. I wonder how he put up with people making excuses not to follow Him right to His face.

It must have been especially difficult to be humble when Satan tempted Him. Why didn't he just say, "I'm God's son, so how do you think that you have anything I want, you fallen angel? You are burnt toast and have nothing for me." How could he let people spit on him, yank out His beard and beat on him? How did he take that whipping and crucifixion and ask God to forgive the people who did it to him? Jesus had the strength to put up with all of that, and I wish that I did. We don't look at being humble as a valued commodity in our society. We think loud and proud is where it's at, and when I'm hurt or disappointed repeatedly, loud and proud is where I'm at too.

***Dear God Almighty,
I know that Your strength involves more love than might. Your unlimited power is under perfect control. I am glad that you loved me more than you wanted to show me who was boss. Help me to love _____ more than I want to throw all his/her failures and deceptions into his/her face. Teach me to forgive when I am deeply disappointed. Teach me to be humble when I want to roar my***

disapproval. Help me to call out to You when it hurts, and show that example to the addict I love. Help me not to lash out. Heal _____ and break the chains of addiction. If s/he was any other sort of slave, I would feel deeply sorry for him/her. But since s/he chooses this repeatedly, I forget that chains are not easily broken in most cases. Let the chains fall off of _____ like they fell off of Peter in prison. And if that is not Your will, let me love and forgive _____ like Hosea forgave his wife, and like you forgive me–time after time. Let the words of my mouth and the meditations of my heart glorify You every day. Teach us your love and forgiveness. Heal us, Lord. In Jesus' name I pray. Amen.

DAY 18- THE LUST OF THE EYES

James 4:1-2 From whence come wars and fightings among you? Come they not hence, even of your lusts that war in your members? Ye lust, and have not...

Most people agree that addiction to drugs, gambling or alcohol is a bad thing, but many consider pornography to be a victimless crime. Unfortunately, we are reaping a terrible harvest from the prevalence of porn in our society. Even worse, it is becoming more acceptable in the mainstream, and younger and younger children are being exposed to it. It is shocking to note how many rapists and sexual predators of every stripe were exposed to pornography at a young age. Like every addiction, the kids pay the price—and then some.

Matthew 5:29 (Jesus said,) "And if thy right eye offend thee, pluck it out, and cast it from thee: for it is profitable for thee that one of thy members should perish, and not that thy whole body should be cast into hell."

Did Jesus pluck out the eyes of anybody during His ministry? No, he healed the blind. But His message is clear. It is better to go through life partially blind than to throw away God's blessings. Most of the gifts that we receive in this life will not last forever. God's gift of forgiveness and adoption into His family will. Nothing whatsoever can snatch us out of His hand. What does that mean for the addicts we love? It means that there is always hope. People with hope can withstand a whole lot more adversity than they think they can. Hope promises a better tomorrow. I have always questioned Paul's sanity when he thanked God for suffering. I can see how his experiences would show him the value of suffering over time, but if I can go through this life with as little pain as possible I will do it. Paul says that suffering results in perseverance, which leads to hope. But I don't want to go through all that just to have hope. How about the God of hope just gives me some? He's generous.

It grieves me that an addict I love is in a terrible place. His life has been threatened by drug dealers more than once, but that still didn't cure him. What will it take? How can he tell himself that he isn't hurting anybody when it is so obvious that he is?

Dear Father in Heaven,
We need a big dose of hope right now. Life has not been easy, and it is wearing on us all. Help us to walk in the path of righteousness. Help us to remember that You have given us all the tools we need to flee temptation. Help us to have the wisdom to know which path to take and to make the right choices. Help those around us not to suffer when we fall. There is a purpose in all suffering, Lord. Help us to remember that. Help us not to become discouraged and give up. Give us the peace that passes understanding. Fill us with Your grace, peace and hope. Break the chains of addiction and heal _____. Heal all those who have given up. Heal those who are hurting or discouraged—especially the children. I pray for the persecuted and the downtrodden, that they may have hope as well. Thank You for all Your blessings, and help us to remember how blessed we truly are. Thank You for giving us what we need when we need it. In Jesus' name I pray. Amen.

DAY 19- A PRAYER FOR COMFORT

An addict I loved died too young. It wasn't his drug of choice that killed him. It was alcohol and a treacherous road. Only months later, his oldest son died from a drug overdose. The shock and pain I felt was nothing compared to that of his family. My heart grieved for them, and for the dad he would never be again. When I was nineteen, this man and another friend convinced me that I needed to give my life to Jesus Christ. At the time, he was one of my best friends. He introduced me to Christian music, and he was a man on fire for the Lord. How could he have fallen so far? Why did the devil and his addiction have so much power over him? This side of heaven, we will likely never know.

Why did Solomon, who had the foresight to ask God for wisdom instead of riches end his life worshipping rocks and build an altar to Molech? Molech received human sacrifice—innocent babies. David, a man after God's own heart, committed murder and adultery. Why is evil so easy to do?

After he finished eating his last supper with his friends, Jesus had a few things to say to Simon Peter, one of his three closest friends on earth.

And the Lord said, Simon, Simon, behold Satan hath desired to have you, that he may sift you as wheat: But I have prayed for thee, that thy faith fail not: and when thou art converted, strengthen thy brethren. Luke 22:31-32

Jesus goes on to tell Simon that he will deny him three times before the rooster crows. A few verses later, Jesus tells his disciples to pray that they won't fall into temptation, and they go to sleep instead—twice. When the soldiers come, all his friends desert Jesus except one. That one denies he ever knew him shortly thereafter, and the Lord heard him do it. According to Luke, Jesus looked straight at Peter as the rooster crowed. Talk about being betrayed! It seems to be easy for man to be faithless, but it hurts us all the same.

Dear Lord,

I know that You have been betrayed by those you love most. I also know that there are times when I am weak, and so is the addict I love. I am asking you to strengthen both me and _____, that we will be able to do Your will day after day, year after year. When _____ lets me down, or lets people we love down, help me to remember that You desire mercy more than sacrifice. You are a great example of how to love through the pain, even pain worse than I can imagine. Fill us with Your Spirit and Your power. When things look impossible, show us that you are the God of second chances. Pray for us, that Satan will not sift us like wheat. When we are faithless, remind us that You are faithful. When we are hurt by the consequences of sin, help us to run to Your arms for comfort. Help us to love when we feel betrayed.

You promise to give us good things if we ask. Give us peace, self-control and a sound mind. When death rears its ugly head, remind us that you have already defeated death, and that this life is not all there is. Take away the spirit of fear and break the chains of addiction. In Jesus' name I pray. Amen.

DAY 20- A PRAYER FOR SAFETY

Is. 43:2 When thou passest through the waters, I will be with thee; and through the rivers, they shall not overflow thee: when thou walkest through the fire, thou shalt not be burned; neither shall the flame kindle upon thee.

An addict I love lived in his car for months during a winter that reached record-breaking cold temperatures. He had a job and a family that loved him. He chose to live in his car because he didn't want to waste money on rent when he could spend it on alcohol. I wonder how many people are living on the streets now that never saw the lengths to which that first drink would take them. I know that some alcoholics don't choose to have their first drink. It comes in the womb or in a baby bottle as unthinkable as that seems. There is so much in our world today that is incredibly evil.

Addicts run in circles that can include deadly, dangerous people. At times, they are easy prey. It is a scary thing the love a person who runs to high crime areas to satisfy their predilections. An addict I love was almost killed by gang members twice within a year and it still did not cure him. In addition, their contact with dangerous people can put their loved ones in peril, even when the loved ones have no idea that they may become a target.

***Dear Father in Heaven,**
Watch over the addict I love. Help _____ to keep him/herself from dangerous situations even in the midst of folly. Have mercy on the addict I love. Provide the tools so that the devil doesn't win today. Protect the family of the addict I love as well. Help us to be strong and to always be on the side of righteousness. Help us to gently but firmly let the addict we love know that if the law is broken, it will be reported. Help us to remind the addict we love that there is no room for that lifestyle near*

the children, the elderly or anybody who can be preyed upon by those involved in spreading that poison. Lord, please protect the safety of the addict I love, of his/her family, friends, and of the officers or medical staff s/he may come in contact with. Lord, if part of the problem is mental illness, let it be diagnosed and properly treated. Give his/her body strength. Protect the lives involved in this tragic situation and give me wisdom enough to keep from encouraging this in any way. Dear Lord, we know that actions have consequences. In your mercy and love, let those consequences be for the good of the addict I love—as well as those who depend on him/her. Break the chains of addiction and let _____ find the joy of the Lord. In Jesus name I pray. Amen.

DAY 21- A PRAYER OF REJOICING

And it shall come to pass, that whosoever shall call on the name of the LORD shall be delivered... Joel 2:32

Luke 19:10 (Jesus said,) "For the Son of man is come to seek and to save that which was lost."

He shall call on me, and I will answer him: I will be with him in trouble; I will deliver him, and honour him. Psalm 91:15

Americans are very proud of their self-sufficiency. We say that God helps those who helps themselves as if it's Scripture. Sometimes there is only a Spiritual answer to a hurtful situation. If I doubt the power of God Almighty, I only need to look out over the ocean, or up at the sky—day or night. God is bigger than my problems, and the Lord of all creation can certainly do all things. He can save the addict I love, and I praise Him for it.

Six times a year, a group from my church leads a service at the Mission of Hope in Mobile, AL. I started to go because of what Brother Miller (who now resides in Glory) and the staff did for an addict I love. But as the years go by, I have seen other friends, former students, and men who looked so gaunt and sickly that I didn't know how long they would make it blessed by this ministry. I know that there are those with more degrees and education than I have that would scoff at the idea that a faith-based program is any more than a psychological stop-gap, but I have seen miracles done in men's lives. I am all for medicine and for treatment, but I will not deny what I have seen the power of God do through this ministry. The man that leads our services is a former drug addict and alcoholic who has been clean since 1988. Several other men from my church who sing with us are former alcoholics. I pray that one day the addicts I love will join us there (or in Heaven, as the case may be) singing, "Victory in Jesus."

One of my best friends is a former drug addict. If you look at her, you would never guess that she was anything but the kindest, most generous Christian lady you have ever met. But even after twenty years of being straight, she says that every once in a while she gets a taste in the back of her throat that reminds her of her days of drug use. Just as quickly, she dismisses it and goes on. Another one of my best friends is a former alcoholic. One night she almost died from alcohol poisoning and decided that she was done drinking. She has never looked back. The stories of these two ladies and so many others let me know that there is a future and a hope for the addict I love. God is good and He loves all of His children and wants them to be free. His salvation is open to all, addict or not, and praise is the natural outpouring of thankfulness for His gift.

Dear Father in Heaven,
I know that You already know how this situation is going to turn out, and you offer salvation to all. You hold us in the palm of your hand and You will not leave us or forsake us.

I praise You for Your love. I praise You for Your mercy. I praise You for Your salvation. I praise You for Your tenderness. I praise You for Your provision. I praise You for Your healing. I praise You for Your blessings. I praise You for Your beautiful creation. I praise You for those I love. I praise You for a future and a hope. I praise You for my freedom. I praise You for Your patience. I praise You because I am Yours. Lord, I praise you for breaking the chains of addiction and healing _____. I praise You for all you have done for me that I don't even know about. I praise You for Your protection. I praise You for Your instruction. I praise Your for sending me godly friends who will pray with me and for me. I praise You for my health. I praise You for Your Word. I praise You for showing me the armor of God. I praise You for teaching me humility and self-control. I praise You for the children. I praise You for the correction.

I will praise You, God, even when it hurts so much that my eyes are swollen from crying, and my heart feels like it will burst. I will praise You in all things because in You I place my trust. I trust You with those I love! In Jesus' name I pray. Amen.

DAY 22- THE LOVING FATHER

Is. 49:15 Can a woman forget her sucking child, that she should not have compassion on the son of her womb? Yea, they may forget, yet will I not forget thee.

I have often heard that each person's view of God is affected by the behavior of his or her human father on earth. I certainly hope that is not the case with me because my dad suffers from hereditary mental illness, brain damage and a bitter, unforgiving spirit. My dad did not abuse me, but living with him was no picnic. I have had friends whose fathers make my dad look like Dad of the Year. Some mothers are no prize either. Even when people have great parents, the children can have an unforgiving, bitter spirit. As a teacher in an alternative school, I often saw the results of broken families. It is likely that social workers and police officers could fill many books with sad stories of the results of a society that has turned its back on God's standard and embraced the shifting sand. I have heard terrible stories of parents who enjoyed torturing their own children or who did nothing to protect their children from abuse of every stripe imaginable. Families are in trouble, little ones are suffering, and the outlook is bleak.

Jesus knew the extent of human selfishness when He told the story of the prodigal son. It was an insult for that child to ask for his inheritance while his father was still alive. It was even worse that he frittered the money away on things that were disgraceful and worthless. But when the boy came to his senses, Jesus painted the perfect picture of a loving father. This man *ran* to his son when he saw him coming. Jewish men didn't run. The father had been insulted and robbed, but all he saw was the child he'd feared was dead walking toward home. No matter how tragic your childhood was, Jesus wants us to know that there is a father who will run to meet you no matter what you have done. He will put his ring on your finger, cover you with his best robe and throw a party when you come home.

Dear Lord,

You know that some people have embraced their addiction because of a tragic childhood. Some addicts have toxic families that they will not stay away from, or cannot for whatever reason. In a world full of abuse and sorrows, You know every need. You know what our souls cry out for, Lord. You know how to heal the addicted ones. You can send help for the children who are suffering—help us to answer the call if that is Your will. You have the answers to the questions that leave us quaking with grief. You have the power to heal and to restore. You offer mercy to those who do wrong, even if they wait until the last minute like the thief on the cross. You can break the chains of addiction. You can set the captive free. You can heal the broken heart. You can set our feet upon the solid rock of your love. You can save a life that is about to be snuffed out. You can reach down and heal a wounded child or a tortured soul. Father, wrap your loving arms around us in our time of need. Help the addict I love to let go of the grief of the past. Heal him/her from the pain, even the pain of his/her own making. Run to the addict I love and bring him/her into the feast. Show Your riches, grace and love. Have mercy on me and mine, Lord. You say where two or more are gathered in Your name, You are there. Well, it's me and Your Holy Spirit here, Lord, and I'm asking for You to work a mighty miracle in the life of the addict I love. Raise him/her from the depths of despair, and bring him/her into the light of your love. Help me to be faithful to pray, to show Your love and mercy, and to walk with you each day. Father, thank you for loving me even more than I can imagine. Let _____ know that you love him/her more than s/he can ever measure—without condition. Let _____ accept your free gift of love and forgiveness and come into your kingdom even now. In Jesus' name I pray. Amen.

DAY 23- THE PRIDE OF LIFE

These six things doth the LORD hate: yea, seven are an abomination unto him: A proud look, a lying tongue, and hands that shed innocent blood, an heart that deviseth wicked imaginations, feet that be swift in running to mischief, a false witness that speaketh lies, and he that soweth discord among brethren. Prov. 6:16-19

Pride goeth before destruction, and an haughty spirit before a fall. Prov. 16:18

For by grace are ye saved through faith; and that not of yourselves, it is the gift of God—Eph. 2:8

There has been a lot of discussion about what the first sin was, but since the pride of Satan got him thrown out of heaven, it is a logical conclusion that pride was the first sin. Pride keeps us from getting help or even admitting there's something amiss. Pride keeps secrets; pride allows terrible wrongs to occur. Pride is the opposite of what makes Christians different—mercy, compassion and love. Pride kept me from sharing the addict I love's problem with my closest friends because I feared what they would say and do.

But my prideful assumption was mistaken. I had people who would pray with us and for us. For years I didn't trust them enough to tell the truth. Pride whispers that I am better than the addict I love, and I really do not need that weight hanging around my neck. Pride says that I am too good for this whole situation; I am nobody's servant. I deserve better, and more, more, more! Pride even got God's people to trade the power of Almighty God for mere logic. We stopped trying to win people to Christ, and tried to reason with them instead. I never realized what a foolish plan this was until I tried being logical with an addict. The power of my reasonable arguments did nothing for him. I could sit up for weeks on end thinking up great reasons why he didn't need his drug of choice, but it just never worked. In my pride I didn't realize that only the God of creation, the God who owns the cattle on a thousand hills, the Savior who died for me and for the addict I love has the power to heal and to restore.

Grace is a free gift that can change everything if we will only accept it. It can give the power of God to those who are going down for the third time. It is the promise of eternity with our loving God, and it cannot be earned. It must simply be received. I know there are those who are thinking, "Crutch!" but what better crutch is there? Almost every person I've heard scoffing about those Christians who need a crutch was an alcoholic. At least my crutch won't leave me lying in my vomit or dead. If the addict I love is leaning on the power of Almighty God instead of the bondage of his addiction, he is in a much better place. Oh, that he would lean on Jesus instead of the drug that enslaves him!

Dear Father in Heaven,
Save us from the pride that makes us less than we should be, or that makes us believe that we are more than we are. Pride tells us to do it on our own. Pride puts the wrong god on the throne. Don't let us believe lies just because they sound reasonable. Show us your grace and love. Teach us mercy and gentleness when we want justice. Let us know that the power of a brain goes only so far, but Your power is unlimited. Send us Your wisdom, and teach us to speak the truth in love. Help us to lift our eyes to You when we just want to cut and run. Give us the boldness to face the truth and the wisdom to know what to do with it. Break the chains of addiction. Heal the addict I love. In Jesus' name I pray. Amen.

DAY 24- JESUS WEPT

I hate to cry. Crying is weak. It leaves salty red trails down my cheeks and my eyes stay red for much too long afterward. If there is one person who is a master at making me cry, it is the addict I love. Oh, I hold out for weeks, even months at a time. Then the dam breaks and I let it all out. If God holds all my tears in his hand, he must have a good bit of saltwater in there by now.

Matthew 5:4 (Jesus said,) *"Blessed are they that mourn: for they shall be comforted."*

I must admit that it is a relief to let the flood of tears loose sometimes. It usually happens in church, so there can be a nice, big audience for my loss of control. But if I can't cry when my church family surrounds me, when can I cry?

If crying didn't have a purpose, why did the Lord cry? He cried when he saw his friends mourn for Lazarus though he would raise him again shortly thereafter. He cried over Jerusalem and the shining city on a hill it was meant to be. Then, shortly before He died, Jesus told the women of Jerusalem not to weep for him, but for their children. Notice that He didn't say not to cry, just not to cry for Him. Tears have their value, even when we are ashamed to cry or tired of crying.

Dear Lord,
__I feel like I have a water tower full of tears, and my heart is so heavy, Lord. This situation seems hopeless and it hurts so much to watch _____ make one destructive choice after another. It hurts to watch others hurt, and it seems like such a waste. What a life _____ could have had without the bondage of his/her addiction. How many of his/her loved ones grieve for the person s/he could be right now, for the abundant life s/he could have had. How hard it is to watch the one I love so__

much destroy him/herself. The worst thing is, s/he doesn't think it's all that bad, doesn't see the pain or even realize the extent of his/her bondage. His/her conscience is seared with a hot iron, and there seems to be no way out. But You are a God of mercy and restoration. You gave Israel chance after chance to follow you, even when they did terrible things. You offer forgiveness and healing even now. You healed many afflictions right before you said, "Blessed are they that mourn, for they shall be comforted." Comfort us. Wrap your arms around this family, Lord. Let _____ accept your free gift. Heal these hearts full of pain and wipe every tear from our eyes. Hold us close to you, Lord, as we walk through each day. Break the chains of addiction. In Jesus' name I pray. Amen.

DAY 25- PRAYER FOR PROVISION

Psalm 69:1-3 Save me, O God; for the waters are come in unto my soul. I sink in deep mire, where there is no standing: I am come into deep waters, where the floods overflow me. I am weary of my crying: my throat is dried: mine eyes fail while I wait for my God.

An addicted young man was given a chance to go into rehabilitation instead of prison. He went to a residential program, graduated, and was clean for three years. He was working and living at home, saving for a house. A friend of the family stopped by one day and the young man's mother burst into tears. Her son was using drugs again, and all of his money was gone. He looked terrible, but was still holding onto his job—barely. Both ladies prayed and spread the word to their friends and family to pray as well. Shortly thereafter, a manager at the place pulled the young man aside and told him that he, too, had been addicted to drugs. He told the young man that he had put his life back together and was now running things instead of running from things. He offered the young man a way to receive treatment and still keep his job and he took it. Both ladies are convinced that the prayers of this mother and her friends are what brought this kind manager into the young man's life. He is now completely drug-free and has never gone back to his old life.

James 5:16 Confess your faults one to another, and pray one for another, that ye may be healed. The effectual fervent prayer of a righteous person availeth much.

Jesus said that even evil people know how to give good gifts to their children, so how much more will God give those who ask. Tap into the power of being a child of the Living God. Ask Him for the desires of your heart. You cannot surprise or shock God; He's seen it all. Be honest and do not give up. His timing is certainly not ours, but He is faithful.

Dear Father in Heaven,
I know that You want what is best for us in this situation. It kills me that _____ can go so long without drugs/alcohol/porn/gambling/bulimia and then jump right back into the cesspool. Heal this situation, Father. Help the addict I love to erect barriers that will keep him/her from what takes them over so completely. Keep the bad influences away and help _____ to find healthy influences and friends. If there is any way that I am contributing to this situation, show me where so I can change it. If there is any way to help the addict I love to conquer this thing, help me to be there—ready to fight for the one I love. Help me to be faithful to pray each time my thoughts turn to this situation, Lord. You said that if we ask, believing, you will give us the desires of our heart. The desire of my heart is that _____ will be cured of the addiction that is ruining his/her life. Do not let the addict I love from his/her bad choices. Restore what has been taken, and heal his/her body. In Jesus' precious name I pray. Amen.

DAY 26- WHERE IS THE FRUIT?

Gal. 5:22-23- But the fruit of the Spirit is love, joy, peace, longsuffering, gentleness, goodness, faith, meekness, temperance: against such there is no law.

The fruit on my tree doesn't seem to be ripening. In fact, I feel like it's rotting off bit-by-bit. Every time it seems like I just might have a good harvest, something comes along and shakes my tree. The addict I love has gone years at times without falling into his addiction. Then suddenly, without warning, the money starts to disappear again. The little grin he gets when he lies starts to show up. The stories start to change.

I don't want to walk away; I want to run. Who can love somebody bent on self-destruction and full of foolishness? Not me. And joy? How can there be joy in the midst of turmoil? The joy of the Lord is my strength, and that joy has been stolen from me and given to some South American drug lord one time too many. I can't be peaceful or self-controlled when I am furious because he looks me right in the eyes and lies without blinking. I'm sick of being faithful while he runs toward destruction. Goodness and gentleness were smashed to bits about five lies ago, and I'm certainly not going to be kind to somebody who doesn't love his kids more than his addiction.

Or can I? How is it that every time the addict I love falls into his addiction, I fall too? I'm not going to let the enemy have two victories. I cannot be a loving example to children already hurt by one person failing if I refuse to use the Holy Spirit's gifts. What has malice ever gotten us? I just picture the devil sitting over in a corner rolling with laughter as I scream out my frustration. He's not winning this time.

Dear Lord Almighty,
I really need help right now to love _____. S/he has let me down again—and not just me, but others who need her/him. S/he is needlessly destroying so many lives

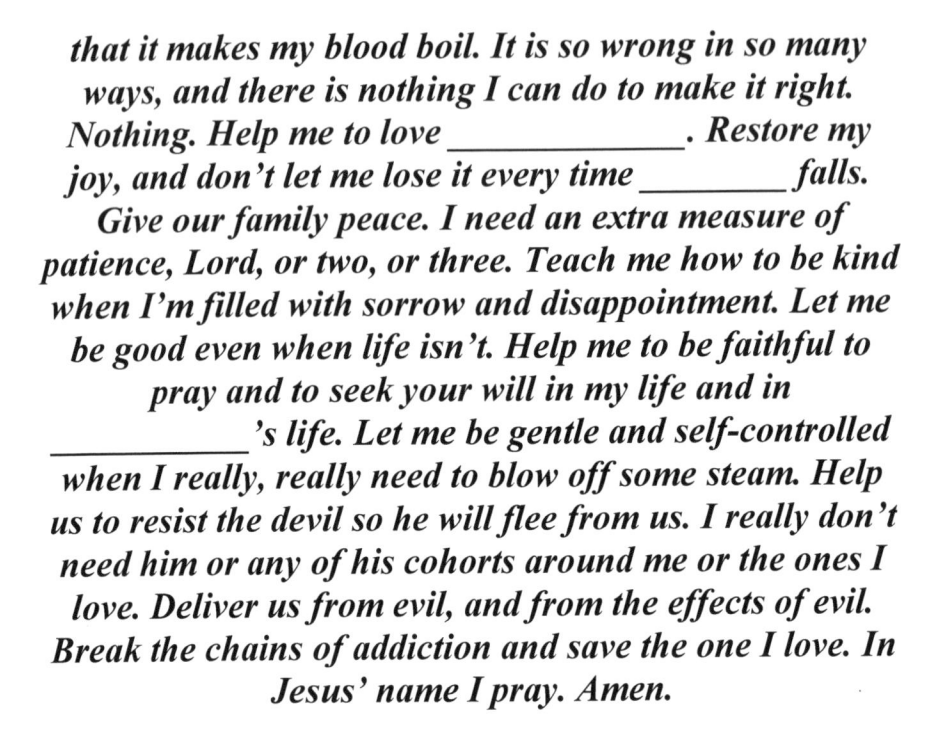

that it makes my blood boil. It is so wrong in so many ways, and there is nothing I can do to make it right. Nothing. Help me to love _____. Restore my joy, and don't let me lose it every time _____ falls. Give our family peace. I need an extra measure of patience, Lord, or two, or three. Teach me how to be kind when I'm filled with sorrow and disappointment. Let me be good even when life isn't. Help me to be faithful to pray and to seek your will in my life and in _____'s life. Let me be gentle and self-controlled when I really, really need to blow off some steam. Help us to resist the devil so he will flee from us. I really don't need him or any of his cohorts around me or the ones I love. Deliver us from evil, and from the effects of evil. Break the chains of addiction and save the one I love. In Jesus' name I pray. Amen.

DAY 27- PRAISE DURING OUR SORROW

Habakkuk 3:17-18 Although the fig tree shall not blossom, neither shall fruit be in the vines; the labour of the olive shall fail, and the fields shall yield no food; the flock shall be cut off from the fold, and there shall be no herd in the stalls; yet I will rejoice in the LORD, I will joy in the God of my salvation.

Even the most hardened murderer can find a criminal "worse" than he is. He'll point to a child molester or similar abuser and figure he is not such a bad guy, not really. It is so easy for people to rationalize their behavior by pointing to somebody worse. Addicts have this down to a science. Habakkuk didn't think that Israel should be punished by the Chaldeans because they were so much worse. But God didn't use the same measure that Habakkuk did. Eventually, he comes around and admits that no matter what, he accepts God's judgment because he knows that God is just. He knew even then that the Savior was coming, and He was coming for Habakkuk and all those he loved.

Then I think of the story of a woman who felt sympathy for a butterfly trying to escape its cocoon. She pulled away the pieces that the butterfly was struggling with, not knowing that the butterfly's wings needed that struggle to be made strong enough to fly. She actually hurt the beautiful creature she was trying to help. I know better than to rescue the addict I love from the consequences of his actions, but I expect God to keep me from all the struggles that make me strong enough to fly. Ouch.

Dear God Almighty,
There is a place in my heart that deeply grieves for the addict I love. There is so much loss and heartache in this situation. Each time it seems that we are making progress and stepping in the right direction, _____ jumps back three steps. I am so sorry for the wo/man s/he could have

been and for all of the hurt that s/he has brought upon the people who love him/her most. S/he is missing out on so much and watching _____ throw away a promising future makes me want to dump a thousand tears into God's hand. Protect and heal the addict I love. Give us hope when it looks like there is none. Help us to use each loss to make us appreciate our blessings. When everything seems to be destroyed beyond repair, help us to remember that Your plan will be accomplished in the end. Break the chains of addiction. Let us remember that we came into this world with nothing and we will leave this world with the same. Help us to remember that the Savior has already come, and the war is already won. Help us to thank You for Your provision and ask for Your blessings daily. Let us never grow weary of doing good. I love you, Lord, and ask for a mighty work for the addict I love. In Jesus' name I pray. Amen.

DAY 28- PRAYER FOR THE ADDICT THAT I HAD TO WALK AWAY FROM

1 Cor. 5:5 …To deliver such an one unto Satan for the destruction of the flesh, that the spirit may be saved in the day of the Lord Jesus.

1 Tim. 5:8 But if any provide not for his own, and especially for those of his own house, he hath denied the faith, and is worse than an infidel.

Matt. 18:17 And if he shall neglect to hear them, tell it unto the church: but if he neglect to hear the church, let him be unto thee as an heathen man and a publican.

I have a friend who knows the word of God, but because she saw a great wrong go unpunished in the church, she doesn't trust His people very much. As a young woman, she knew a sweet and generous Christian woman who worked in her same building. This woman was the picture of kindness and gentleness. She would often come into the building with a black eye courtesy of her husband. He was a deacon in a Bible-believing church, but the church members turned a blind eye to this woman's plight and let it go on. I can't blame my friend for being disenchanted with God's people. Timothy clearly spells out what a deacon should be, and there are many examples in the Bible of a woman whom God protects. The bride of Christ should do the same. The Bible also says that a husband and wife are one flesh, and that the man should take care of his wife like he does his own body. Husbands are commanded to love their wives as Christ loved the church. Christ gave his life for the church. This example of a church not following God's discipline was a terrible example to those who saw it happen. We know people are watching, so we should be careful to follow God's word. Even if it is a popular or powerful person who is doing the wrong.

As much as it hurts, there is a time to walk away from an addict. Especially in the case of you or the children being in danger. If an addict is repeatedly rescued from the consequences of his or her sin, why should he or she stop? If an addict has no financial incentive to refrain, the dangerous behavior is being encouraged. I do not want to stand before the Lord and admit that I helped an addict I love kill himself. If you read each of the above sets of verses in context, you will see that the purpose of walking away from an addict is so s/he can be restored. Even the selfish, worldly prodigal son understood his failings after wallowing in the pigsty for long enough. And starving in the pigsty was what he needed. Tough love is sometimes the only option for those who refuse to face facts. Why do you think the Bible says those who will not work should not eat? Sometimes God has to get somebody's attention the hard way as much as it hurts. Of course, this decision should be bathed in prayer. Even when there is peace about the decision, the pain will still be fierce. But as long as an addict has breath, he or she can change.

Dear Almighty God,
Please provide a way for me to escape the situation with _____. Give me the strength to cut all ties, financial and otherwise, to allow _____ to see that s/he needs help. Only You can heal this situation, Lord. Give me the wisdom to know which direction to go. Give me the resources to protect myself and my loved ones from _____. Heal the addict I love, and break the chains of addiction. Please provide what we all need in this situation. My heart is broken, Lord, and I know that Yours is too. Keep us safe, and let us walk with you each day. In Jesus' name I pray. Amen.

DAY 29- PRAYER FOR WISDOM & UNDERSTANDING

(Jesus said) "The thief cometh not, but for to steal, and to kill, and to destroy; I am come that they might have life, and that they might have it more abundantly. John 10:10

If any of you lack wisdom, let him ask of God, that giveth to all men liberally, and upbraideth not; and it shall be given him. James 1:5

Sometimes loving an addict seems completely hopeless. I am fighting against the will of a person completely caught in the web of addiction as well as against the spiritual realm. Satan is a liar and the father of it. He is also an angel with more power than any human. He comes to kill, steal and destroy. The addict I love seems to find every imaginable resource to get his/her hands on what they want. How can I fight all that? Am I really supposed to be fighting the good fight of faith? After all, I'm not a young preacher (see 1 Tim. 6:12) so why should I bother? Oh, it's that whole "I love an addict" thing again. I love several addicts, and the list of them just keeps growing as I age. Great. I am so glad that Jesus came to bring a full life to people because every time I try to outsmart the addict I love, or reason with him/her—no matter what I try—the addiction wins nearly every time. I look at those who have been healed and I wonder what the formula is. Why do some abandon their family, destroy everything around them and eventually kill themselves, while others learn to live without the alcohol, pornography, drugs, (or whatever) and live to a ripe old age? If only I knew the right buttons to push, I wouldn't have to spend so much time on my knees crying out to God. But maybe that is the point. The addict I love isn't the only one with lessons to learn. Teach me Your ways, oh Lord, and show me Your paths.

Dear Father in Heaven,
I would love a healthy dose of wisdom right now. Please show me how to best pray for the addict I love. Please give me the wisdom to do all within my power to point

him/her to You. Fill me with your Spirit, and guide my steps each day, Lord. Every time I want to complain, let me turn to You in prayer. Every time I am afraid or angry or feel like things are hopeless, let me tap into Your strength. I pray all these things for the addict I love, too. Smash every lie to pieces. Lord, I don't know why s/he chooses the things s/he does. I don't understand what put _____ in this position or why this web is so unbreakable. Please don't let injustice reign in this situation. I know that You can give him/her the power to walk away from the things that are stealing his/her life away. Please break the chains of addiction, Lord. Thank you, Father, for all of the blessings that you have rained down upon us, and please add to them the peace that passes all understanding. Bless us and keep us; shine Your face upon us and give us peace. In Jesus' name I pray. Amen.

DAY 30- I WILL PRAISE GOD

Psalm 148:1-14; Praise the LORD
Praise ye the LORD. Praise ye the LORD from the heavens; praise him in the heights. Praise ye him all his angels: praise ye him all his hosts. Praise ye him, sun and moon: praise him all ye stars of light. Praise him, ye heavens of heavens, and ye waters that be above the heavens. Let them praise the name of the LORD: for he commanded, and they were created. He hath also stablished them forever and ever: he hath made a decree which shall not pass. Praise the LORD from the earth ye dragons, and all deeps. Fire, and hail: snow and vapour; stormy wind fulfilling his word: Mountains and all hills; fruitful trees, and all cedars; Beasts and all cattle; creeping things and flying fowl: Kings of the earth, and all people; princes, and all judges of the earth; Both young men, and maidens; old men and children: Let them praise the name of the LORD: for his name alone is excellent; his glory is above the earth and heaven. He also exalteth the horn of his people, the praise of all his saints; even of the children of Israel, a people near unto him. Praise ye the LORD.

It is hard to praise when I worry, but it is harder to worry when I praise. Jesus asked who could make himself taller by worrying about his height. He reminded us of the beauty of the lilies, and how much God desires to give us good gifts. If there is one thing that I have learned from loving an addict, it is that my God is bigger than any addiction or problem or pain. Even though some addicts I love are not healed, and it seems my prayers are not answered, I know that God has a plan for our lives. The "horn" in verse 14 is a symbol of strength. I know God has strength beyond what I can comprehend, and that He has this under control. If rocks can praise God, if God takes care of even common things like birds and wildflowers, I certainly can praise him—and depend on His strength and provision even in the worst of times. After all, I don't have to eat worms and beetles to survive.

Dear Lord, my Father,
I will praise You. I praise You for healing the addict I love. I praise You for the beauty of your creation. I praise You for the fact that I was born in this rich, free land. I praise You that I have such value to the King of Kings. I praise You for my education, my health, my talents, and for all the people I love whom You have given me. I praise you for restoring what the locust has eaten. I praise You for your correction and teaching. I praise You for breaking the chains of addiction in the addict I love. I praise You because I trust You. I praise You for Your mercy and love. I praise You because You are my strength and my song. I praise You because You care. I praise You for all the blessings that I don't even know You have rained down on me and mine. In Jesus' name I pray. Amen.

DAY 31- PRAYER WHEN YOU ARE THE ADDICT

"I am not a terrible person, and I don't mean to hurt others. I just need it," said the addict I love.

Psalm 69:16-18 Hear me, O LORD; for thy lovingkindness is good: turn unto me according to the multitude of thy tender mercies. And hide not thy face from thy servant; for I am in trouble: hear me speedily. Draw nigh unto my soul and redeem it: deliver me because of mine enemies.

Psalm 63:6-7 When I remember thee upon my bed, and meditate on thee in the night watches. Because thou hast been my help, therefore in the shadow of thy wings will I rejoice.

The guilt and shame of being an addict is likely an agonizing, piercing reality for those who are trapped in the cycle of dependency. Despite your best efforts, you fail. And you fail again. Then one more time. It seems that nobody will ever trust you again. You don't even trust yourself. But there is hope. Jesus came to seek and save the lost, the heavy burdened, and the beaten down. Yes, failure has plagued you, but greater is He who is in you than he who is in the world. There is a victory, and many victories coming for those who love and serve the Lord.

1 Cor. 10:13- *There hath no temptation taken you but such as is common to man: but God is faithful, who will not suffer you to be tempted above that ye are able; but will with the temptation also make a way to escape, that ye may be able to bear it.*

But what if I don't stand? What if I fall and fall and fall again? Welcome to life. For all have sinned and fallen short of the glory of God. All of us fall and fail. All of us must ask God for help to walk with Him every day. That's why our life is often called our "walk with God". A walk is one step at a time. What steps can you take to walk away from the chains that bind you? How can you flee temptation? Which safeguards can you put into place to help you to stay on the straight and narrow path? Write a list. Write several.

Brainstorm ideas, and keep trying, leaning on Almighty God as you walk. Never, ever give up. When you feel like you can't take another step, keep walking. Keep praying. Keep studying God's word. Genesis reminds us that God is our Creator who loves us and wants us to walk with Him. Exodus reminds us that even the strongest power on earth cannot survive when it challenges the LORD. Proverbs is full of wisdom. Psalms is full of praise and heartache. Job reminds us that tragedy is not permanent. Jesus reminds us in the Gospels that he has already paid the full price for our sins, and we only need to come to Him when we are weary and heavy-laden. Revelation reminds us that we have the victory already. He will give us rest. Get to know God's love letter. It is your sword. Use it.

Dear Father in Heaven,
Thank You for loving me even more than I can imagine. Thank You that nothing can separate me from the love of God, and that You can reach down and heal me and mine. Lord, I believe You can heal me from my addiction, and from the lengths that I have gone to fulfill my desires. Help my unbelief! Please heal, and restore to me what the locust has eaten and restore any bridges that I have burned. Keep me safe from retaliation from those who are used to profiting from my addiction, Father. I acknowledge you as Lord and Savior. Lead me in Your ways day by day. Break the chains of addiction and give me the strength day by day to do what is right. Heal me from my past, and help me to remember that I am a child of the King of Kings! Even when I feel completely broken, fill me with your Spirit. Help me to remember that my emotions will change, but Your love for me does not. Give me life, and abundant life, overflowing with your love. Help me to walk with You each day, and to hide Your word in my heart so I will not sin against You. You are a lamp unto my feet as I take each step each day. Shine your light and give me wisdom and peace. In Jesus' precious name I pray. Amen.

Made in the USA
Columbia, SC
29 April 2023